A Force That Takes

Edward Ragg

Published by Cinnamon Press
Meirion House,
Glan yr afon,
Tanygrisiau,
Blaenau Ffestiniog,
Gwynedd,
LL41 3SU
www.cinnamonpress.com

The right of Edward Ragg to be identified as the author of this work has been asserted by him in accordance with the Copyright, Designs and Patent Act, 1988. Copyright © 2013 Edward Ragg
ISBN: 978-1-907090-86-8

British Library Cataloguing in Publication Data. A CIP record for this book can be obtained from the British Library.

Designed and typeset in Palatino by Cinnamon Press
Cover from original artwork Vine Stock by Fred De Bailliencourt
© Fred De Bailliencourt, agency: dreamstime.com
Cover design by Jan Fortune

Printed in Poland

Cinnamon Press is represented in the UK by Inpress Ltd www.inpressbooks.co.uk and in Wales by the Welsh Books Council www.cllc.org.uk

Acknowledgments

The author gratefully acknowledges the following publications in which some of these poems first appeared: *Acumen, Envoi, Orbis, Other Poetry, PN Review, Poetry Quarterly, Seam* and *Three Line Poetry.*

'Some Other Mea Culpa' was first published in *Poetry Quarterly* and subsequently collected in *Lung Jazz: Young British Poets for Oxfam* ed. Todd Swift and Kim Lockwood (Cinnamon Press/ Eyewear Publishing, 2012).

'The Entire Scale', 'The Taking of the Capital', 'Waiver' and 'Afterwords' were first published in *Jericho & Other Stories & Poems* ed. Rowan B. Fortune (Cinnamon Press, 2012).

This volume is indebted to the support and encouragement of numerous people, including: Jan Fortune, Michael Schmidt, Carole Baldock, Patricia Oxley, Anne Berkeley, Rod Burns, Glen Lvyers, Amy Wack, Catherine Smith, Colin MacCabe, Brian Cox, Patricia McCarthy, Matthew Welton, Bernard O'Donoghue, Mark Ford, Peter Reading, Mick Imlah, Michael Donaghy, William Logan, Peter Roberts, Susan Cokyll, Charles Altieri, Bart Eeckhout, Nazeer Chowdhury, Sarah Haggarty, Chris Yates, Sarah Cain, Maartje Scheltens, Alex Dougherty, Martin Jones, Jenny Jones, Nick Hanlon, Wang Ao, Eleanor Goodman, Hu Xudong, Yan Li and Denis Mair.

Special thanks are owed to Fongyee Walker, who has nurtured and inspired these poems in innumerable ways, and to the Ragg and Walker families.

This volume is dedicated to the memory of Tedman Littwin, a great teacher.

Contents

Note on Text

Around the time of writing
a cat brushed his knee,

demonstrating for one
and all how the most

resourceful creatures
make their opinions

known in silent messages
surrounding the truth of words.

Homage to Arvo Pärt

I'd say that I have a need to concentrate on each sound... so that every blade of grass would be as important as a flower.

~ *Arvo Pärt on 'Für Alina'*

Two lines walking in the night
of each other or by the daylight sun,

two lines, quite neutral in themselves,
but none other. They are lovers

in the same city or parish lane,
or, walking in the same meadow,

at another hour, have missed
each other quite, quietly passing

over blades and leaves of grass,
almost trod together, as if to say

a blade of grass has the status
of a flower, or at certain hours,

if we walk carefully, will bloom
before our eyes quite unexpectedly,

our feet weary with grass
and the two-step dance.

Two lines walking... it is
essential they never meet singly.

Their minds move upon silence,
as if the entire equation of

their mingling was like the moment
before the conductor's baton

falls, as they seem to
walk in a final embrace,

never quite touching...

The Entire Scale

The impossibility of the city
and globe and the outer
reaches of that globe,

the dull pulse of entirety...
How tempting to say
each life implies

an artistry in the
rear of the actual,
how definitive.

The orange leaves
and the brown leaves
courting in the square...

They define a force
that is spent or
ebbing in the wind.

The winding towers,
the atelier and the rent
scale in the pay of things,

lyric tokens of an
autumnal exchange.
Pianist and typist, too,

are almost seasonal
creatures, as much a man
or woman rehearsing

how the afternoon becomes
darker, how the music sounds
in love with the memory of light.

Walking Backwards

There is a painting of Van Gogh's
of two crabs, more portrait than still life;

or of a single crab upon its back
clipping at the wind,

then righted in the self-same shell,
all pincers and sea-gurgling,

a mere claw's clap to its left
upon a turquoise plateau

none may see...

Because it is an ocean of the table
or verandah of the deep

it ventures slowly backwards to the
yellowest hours, just as tomorrow will be

1889 and scuttling across the ocean floor,
among the bones, the oldest men –

some blind, some mad – will picnic
on the sage counsel of crabmeat.

The countryside of Arles has changed
lately. But they seem to find their way

without caring to look over their shoulders,
without meaning to right their ageing shells.

The Death of Naming

By definition it is a death
coming after the fact,
the butterfly on its needle.

In this crisp winter air,
it is preferable not
to know the names

of things, to watch
the disappearance of
our breath as less

than vapour almost...
The origins of words
are so many cart horses.

To be saddled in their talk
wears a harness no trapeze
artist draws to the wire.

And yet only remembered
speech can make
the use of ignorance.

Outside is China.
Apartments, towers,
the storied factory

air: all return to me
as *lou* or would if I had
need to explain myself –

which today I have not –
hearing the names and
wondering how they got

there if, once they come
to me, I will be alive or lying
in their stead singing almost.

Some Other Mea Culpa

That the wind-wards wise of blame
is a cloak or curtain drape in which

a certain child folds the pleats, I know;
that, walking, if I angle my wrists

neither can you clasp the world in a ball
nor find yourself flying, as if we could

do nothing but flying... That I have
worried about the figures of balances

and less the balance of figures is
a seminal crime and, worse still,

understandable, that it is understandable.
To have clasped, then understood the

innumerable un-understandable things
at first light is, likewise, a crime,

if worth committing, that, also in the
written line they have understood it

or find it understandable, that this too is
a kind of crime I should have committed.

Announcement

The exodus of the city
at festival or as for us

leaving in paragraphs
that are days and sometimes

months... They have a way
of being pronounced.

If it is true that such
changes in our lives

are mostly grief
or if it is undeniable

that they are not,
they live in sentences

that may attain clarity
as what is pronounced...

That is all.

Chongwenmen Market

Its doors are winter coats, dressed for the season
like dumpling wrappers: the snapped dough
rolled in wafer rounds, deft hands cupping
pork mince and scallion into ear-nipped *jiaozi*.
Ahead, river trout squirm on wet marble
like sprung bows as fresh as a definition,
flipping alongside crates of blue crab;
and, fresher still, whole tanks of catfish
plucked from the water in barely a cleaver's drop.
I intone in snail Mandarin the prices of eggs,
pork belly, mutton, counting change in the abacus
of a new speech and would like to say more:
something about the colours of the aubergines,
the less recognized fruits, the tastes of them.

Tsinghua Spring

Purple petals and the cry of the pineapple man
hauling his cart up through the campus gate.
He carves the fruit of his delight or would,
pointing to the sky as if in reach of the mandate
of heaven. Ahead, the pines are *tabulae formis*
and the willows a little green, flanked by pendular
Sophora japonica. They have their badges and much
to say. The students bicycle by, hungrily.

Courtyard and canal, each is still in motion:
the bamboo sways, a girl balances on toe-tips
at the first blossom, the parched earth startles
with colour. Everything forms in the tablet
of my mind as freshly crunched pineapple...
Willow-drape and sprung root: be green.

Reversing Sonnets

After Lavinia Greenlaw's 'Winter Finding'

Until she lights on somewhere to arrive
box-cut hedges in a cul-de-sac drive
smart her sense longing for impatient cliffs
without a view but within a minute
photographed traipsed to know them there the skiffs
the anchored bay the clouds that suddenly fit
the frame of bobbing hulls and blent sea air
how stepping backwards from a wintry edge
is almost to ask 'Is this love?' or care
enough to touch a painted window ledge
as much a cure for seeing as to know
face-to-face the visible betrayal
of winter gone that melting ice will show
the harbour master's hands unfurl the sail

The harbour master's hands unfurl the sail
of winter gone that melting ice will show
face-to-face the visible betrayal
as much a cure for seeing as to know
enough to touch a painted window ledge
is almost to ask 'Is this love?' or care
how stepping backwards from a wintry edge
the frame of bobbing hulls and blent sea air
the anchored bay the clouds that suddenly fit
photographed traipsed to know them there the skiffs
without a view but within a minute
smart her sense longing for impatient cliffs
box-cut hedges in a cul-de-sac drive
until she lights on somewhere to arrive

The Language of Poetry

My father of a morning
bonded to Imperial

Chemical Industries
knew the colours of it,

his delicious *Not necessarily*
and the once imagined

lives of germanium,
gallium and scandium,

his love of the transition
metals and the feeling

compounds sibilant
and numerical in their

trace, rising in the
schoolyard air in

oxides of calm.

Anthem at Morning

How wonderful it would be
in this brightest of mornings

to walk in the clear light
not of possibility

but purpose and to sing
in that same clear light

of the purpose that
in all possibility is today.

Fame

for Emily Dickinson (1830-1886)

An if
became an it   ·
and then a that,

no more than that.

The World Clock

The beauty of synchronicity
is unattainable hope.

I wind the dials, confirm
the digits, in joy of

a precision that fails
regularly. If there were

a synchronicity
of words to sound

how the clocks chime
in the regrettable palaces…

I had imagined for you
a house of stainless steel

from whose vibrations
calibrates every pulsing

heart, at least of a chronic
disposition, not allowing

that the synchronous gaze
will one day finally say

there is no time,
that there is no time…

that the regrettable clocks
in the unattainable palaces

have sprung their mechanisms,
have chimed their last,

or at least strike as precisely
as that hour may sound.

Arriving on the Scene

Perhaps a crowd gathers,
the bystanders first,
then an official

arriving on the scene.
So much easier to depict
than to arrive oneself

or discover oneself arriving,
or to admit the manqué
than accept that tragedy.

That reaching things
has also for us
been difficult

is as much
a matter of approach
as determination,

which is the same.
How I would love
to arrive at a gallery

and stand before
a portrait alone
or as a portrait

of someone arriving,
perhaps unexpectedly,
also to remain standing

unnoticed by those
bystanders to the scene
who among the chatter

and speculation imagine
an official portrait arriving
as if they were there.

The Taking of the Capital

That first winter,
three days of rockets
and fire-crackers

as if the sky was lit
with the nomenclature
of the vivid;

or the city taken siege
by aerial bombardments
of light, sound and

distance – for which
there are no names.
Then the odd incendiary

at the periphery of
observance, as if a
skulking spirit had

tip-toed on the comedy
of ritual combustion
blown out in sound.

Such an offering has
taken the look of things
from what we thought,

in the cinders of a capital
which is not ours nor theirs
in the incense-heavy air.

Waiting Tables in China

Among the young girls waiting
among the young men
in lines of custom waiting

are young boys standing in lines
among young women waiting...
Shouted orders at morning

become shouted orders at night
or among the luncheon hour
in which we find them,

the air fragrant with oil,
garlic sweet from its sheath,
of ginger impounded.

They are the future of the country:
the children of their wages
among schoolchildren

beyond the kitchens.
For, truly, they are waiting,
waiting in lines of custom,

like us, to be served.

Valediction: Or What is Forbidden

Rain over Vancouver,
my night-owl ear two yards
from the windowpane.

Hundreds of feet above
the evening's final
jet engines serenading,

as if nothing were less
possible than to hear
their power without

the rain's stagehand chicanery...
What is stranger than
the absence of a person?

Not absence itself
of which there is none
but many, just as

what is forbidden
must too exist or have
left us no opportunity

except memory, even
this most recent power
of which it is forbidden

to say more, that is poetry...
Your familiar skin, the light
and breath of your smile

somewhere crossing
the dateline, the cataracts
that separate day from day

in the theatre of night
among the jets flowing:
I cannot say that final word

save in songs of water,
darkness, air, your familiar skin
in the night-owl's light inseparable.

Snow in Beijing

Everything is surprised:
new drivers uncertain
of their wheels,

the swishing wiper blades;
children retrieving
their footprints

like first steps;
strays impressed
at their sinking paws.

The gift of the unfamiliar,
if we are to receive it,
is its familiar terms:

the Summer Palace
shot in white, trees
ponderous with ice.

Arid capital, the reception
of your millions is as the
snowfall's persistent padding.

My outstretched palm,
the crowds of snowflakes
collecting there, becomes

your antenna as if,
to your surprise, you had
received us overnight alone.

Declaration

Who understands
as experience

the beauty of someone
seeming; then

the beauty of someone
being, understands

beauty… or is it love?
The bright line

of the hawk at morning,
the bright line

that glides back
to us as someone

is something
one can call hope.

History

By the waters of Luoyang
the faceless Buddhas stand.

The defacing armies,
what figures they unveiled

have no complexion now,
without expression

save for the futility
of their faces

being absent...

Thousands of miniatures
form a figure of resistance

in face of the labour
of destruction,

art that tires
the pummelling hand,

lotus-illuminated,
and, as if by chance,

a rock decorated
in the pattern of peonies

(they say
naturally formed...)

What is natural
in the eyes that remain

and the absent faces?
The water lapping,

the poet's temple
on the farthest bank,

the breeze upon
the waters.

Researchers and Consultants

It may be how the world
looks or is looking toward
of course in our own gazing

choices made feverishly
in the book-stacks for whatever
we were looking it may be

no one has asked us for our
opinions concerning things
or researched desire crossing

the carpets or heavy breaths
in a cork-lined room, though
these too are remarkable indices.

Motives behind questions,
the motives behind those,
are yet more questions

around which possible answers
strangely crowd, how discussion
turns to nothing that is not very

unnecessary, merely unnecessary
like the pedant examining
shoelaces that will never walk.

My study today, the public square,
finds an irresistible Chihuahua
in winter coat consulting an

imitation lawn, happy to ignore
his hapless owner – how are they
thinking? So ineffectually there.

The Meaning of Failure

Who suggests,
as death is absolute,
none will remember

our blunders, oversights,
gaffs in the trade of living
and how we met them

in the sun perhaps less
awkwardly (than we remember)
has not found

the meaning of failure
and its achievements
against the waning day.

If all argument ends
in death, the argument ends.
Yet its very terms

as from a child's world,
if they will have one, is
of argument without end.

Success is so inessential
and failure a condition
in which we may begin

to make again a world,
as when you pour the tea,
you kiss my cheek,

you walk from room
to room moving in a kind
of triumph barely seen.

After Months of Competition

September is only the beginning
of October... Or so she wrote

in her final notes, her twenty-day
blonde hair now silver-edged,

sensing that chill in the air
was her own breath failing.

Somehow as the days grew
shorter there was more

to say and more need
of saying it, but her pages

glared whiter at every turn
for all the fading of summer.

Outside the door-bell hour,
does she start at the thud

of his first, final knock,
arrived with bushels at his breast,

sporting a crown of fallen leaves,
now yellow, now red,

not blazing, delineated,
like a harvest of ideas?

September is the only beginning
of October like a returning sister

who has the edge on her colourful
brother, who, although a little

sad as she stirs the tea is more than
beautiful, as she straightens his leaves,

arranges his pumpkins and gourds,
goes to prepare their last supper.

The Distant Object of Longing Is Also Material

After Yan Li's painting of that title (2008)

Shades of the office towers
and silent malls
and polished plaques

that name one object
or a season
of others,

the underlying sense
of feeling, running
in grooves or rivulets

and the businesses
in whose bricks
or virtual offices

has cracked
that feeling
the underlying sense...

It is not enough
to say I have looked
upon the Fragrant Hills,

my back to the city,
and then turned
to face the TV towers

considering Yan Li
and his painting
of that title

the distant object
of longing
is also material.

The names
upon the plaques
I cannot read

to which
we are longing
2008

now distant
now here belonging
to this material

2008
Harking a new order
which may amount

to more than
disposable plaques
and the silent malls

2008
May amount to something
the like of which

we have never seen.

There Are Certain Heroes

There are certain heroes,
unnoticed in the calendar hour,
who in a recognizable season

walk quietly through country
lanes... asking if there is
a plausible nocturne,

hoping there is, and what
sounds the songs of courage,
what melody courage is.

They have heard the tenor
of lift shafts descending,
the warmth of blood alcohol

at the feasting tables as a voice
acutely speaks. The quietest
poems assume their speech.

They have heard there are
certain heroes, not unlike them,
who, as they pace the meadow

home, arrive at a credible song,
that the nocturnal air is
more than plausible,

the daring ballad a melody
these other heroes, knowing
no heroics, have recognized.

Chateau Musar

We are inoculated to resist.

~ Serge Hochar

The shade of the pergola,
the safest of vineyards, brings
no ripeness to this land.

To be rooted here
is to squat low
yet remain upstanding,

to know that each
juice-taut grape, each
cluster bunch held

is as permeable as skin
yet more symbolic,
that resilience has

no temperature,
survival no sun
except the oldest one.

That There

That there are the secret places
for every life to which it is
only possible to go in person

or in name or by carrying
the look of the time in its feeling
as if it was also there;

that there is no telling
what those feelings are
or where they have carried us

or what remains precisely
secret in having shared
some part of that there

and yet cannot be more ours,
our beautiful secrets, all this
must arise from what stands

between that which is there
and our arriving which remains
for all our thanks a question

of knowing no more than that
that was there or – if we may
ask presently – if this is here.

China

I live in a country
like no other country

in which aspirations
outweigh possibilities

perhaps; as in every
country I know, except

here it is possible
and will continue

every morning
and every night

in a kind of permanence
that endures

or would seem
to be enduring.

Political Poem

I

A quality of light,
of waves or

the sound of water
(whichever the

less abstract)
in tin cans or

dry pails dreaming,
is the shadow

or quality of
objects moving

before that light,
darkening shadows

in the cracked earth
dreaming...

II

The scientist, rightly,
conceives of light

without shadow,
the politician less.

Or is it affluence
in the brightest light

which hides the eye
from shadow

yet may not, poetry
from manor to cottage gate?

III

I might have waited
outside, knowing

this was as much
a decision (if unknowing)

as entering, leaving
or repairing that threshold,

if not for those inside
caught hoisting

the hearth to the
mantelpiece, admiring.

In what gaudy frames
are the portraits hung?

IV

A white man on a desert road…

White men on desert roads…

V

I feel I am rising
in my powers

and having risen
not to have escaped.

VI

Sandalwood: my father
shaving, my father

become me, weighing
lines of reason,

in the scent of sandalwood,
the whole unreasonable day.

VII

We are wary of poems
that announce things

and wary of those
that cannot.

VIII

Falcon of Otago,
they say you are

master surveyor
among the thermals.

For you know there is
neither beauty nor play

without sustenance.

IX

In what frames are
the gaudy portraits hung?

A writer fearing discovery
finds portal upon portal

in multiplying frames.

X

So the wind shifts,
whatever your powers.

Their dreams
are watching us

and what is
without compassion

arriving uninvited
in the smaller hours.

Matinee Breathing

Not the chrome gleam of the cinema roof,
the dark wood offset by the afternoon sun;

not the delicious rip of that half-fondled slip,
unfurled, re-rolled, between finger and thumb;

not the pocketed stub, already souvenir
of whatever's to come; nor even the collector's

guiding arm, proprietorial, a bit absurd,
as if anyone could miss their appointed line.

Not the cocooning darkness either, the scant
audience, the feigned crises in which, still

turning those stubs, battalions of seats
fall over themselves with angles, visions,

their cushion-frayed plots of entangled love
glanced at whatever distance we deign to gaze.

Not even trailer, or pre-view, or featured
presentation or, lastly, the spectral credits

which, to our view, never outstay their welcome,
just as, the usher prowling, we must outlast ours.

Not even the happy accident of that morning word,
matinee, gracing the afternoon's cobalt projections,

as if we had arrived at the truth a little tardily…
It is the first breath outside that comes

like the refreshment of an original breath:
that the world we knew is hardly over,

yet little the same, that we, somehow other now,
are the hero, *are* the victim, the farmer

tilling the plain, the lawyer mouthing, the painter
turning to turpentine again, *are* optative, observant,

knowing that, without us, they – whoever they are –
will never find their rightful places among the stars.

For the Love of

Let the willow blossom
come in May and dust
the streets in intricate floss.

For now I am content
the young women of Beijing
walk arm in arm laughing.

The hair of their necks
has a special quality
for it is not of the willow

nor do they love water
that way touching something
other than the fabric

of this dry, northern breeze
which the men have also
begun to love now they are

comfortable with their virility,
having found a place
in which to be both male

and human, which is man.
They know that make of beauty
here where everything is made.

The hair of their necks
is inseparable, as intricate as
floss, of nothing ulterior

and yet the woman I love,
her Chinese hair now bending
under the cooker hood

has made me forget winter,
the month of May, the willow
trees bending the water's way.

The Philosopher's Bent

Only with fatigue arrive
certain conundrums:

and of the uncertain

The Philosopher and the Lake

At the water's edge
and the smooth edge

of the weathered stone
whose pumice yields

to the water's edge
is not a proposition

yet...

For what is unclear
is not not clear.

But with clarity to speak
and not of the not not

that is nothing
that they say is nothing

must be something:
the stone skipping

or how it leaves the palm,
the air tucked underneath

that thing is
beneath reckoning.

The Lake and the Philosopher

Or is it not
the water

that yields
to the pebble shot

momentarily?
Momentarily, yes,

but the weathered stone
and the earth,

marl that was
all limestone once

all limestone
beneath the waters.

So that he said
To speak not of the not not:

that is too negative
and wary too

of the too positive,
at least what it posits,

seeking a weight
of unusual prowess,

a weathering
at the water's edge,

the prow and the
gentle water lapping...

So that he said.

Triangulation by Spices and Herbs

For a dozen years
I've traced the outline
of your scents.

I open the drawer
of spices and herbs
neatly marked.

Our cinnamon bark –
you remind me –
is Chinese cousin cassia,

so that I recall
cinnamon's curlicued
cheroots, a scrollwork

distinct from the
chipped brittle pieces
fragrant in my hand.

These I mislabel acacia.
But all three are pinpointed
in the aromatics of your mind.

Not that you are infallible.
Take vanilla, for example,
its unwithering fragrance

unsheathed at a knife's point
in seeds you said were sex
or like pheromones

could draw this quivering
heart to pointless weeks
of fully-clothed research.

Vanilla, from the orchid
whose flowers open
to the Melipona bee,

but whose pods could never
travel the world until, like love,
they were pollinated by hand.

I'll match your cassia, love,
with fenugreek and popping
mustard seeds and garam masala

whose combination (and location)
you'll need my body to discover.
Fenugreek, whose buxom

stench is sotolon, common to
the oldest wines of nobly rotten grapes
and the *rancio* of Douro bake.

How sexy and technical
is our spice trail.
The drawer is closing.

So by your body and mind
I am placed in a triangulation
that begins and ends

at the same point (behind
your ears), that for all
the wild herbs by the

highway's verge I have not
set foot from the kitchen
of your heart, its pungent route.

The Indigenous People Are Good
at Hurling Spears

The indigenous people
are good at hurling spears.

That single blade,
its rotating shaft travels

through the departure lounge
among luxury goods

pointed as night
and lands in this

in-flight magazine
in which I read

the indigenous people
are good at hurling spears

which, now I have seen them,
the nose of the plane edging

from the tarmac slightly,
am inclined to agree.

Donkey and Dragon

In heaven they feast on dragon's meat. On earth we eat donkey.

~ *Beijing saying*

I cannot carve a dragon,
not even from stone,

but in the written line
surround them as they

engorge upon the flesh
of that miraculous beast,

gourmets of the
ultimate kingdom...

I am happiest cupping
a donkey's ear or outside

Taiyuan munching the
thin strips in vat-aged

vinegar, knowing this
animal serves so many

needs in the laden hills,
the hoof-trod loess.

The Equation of Need

Clusters in the subway carriages,
an infant bawling. Her father
stands mouthing the softest words.

What pacific speech that koala-like
she encircles his weathered neck?
Sounds. Movement. Someone smiles.

Then his voice inflects, passing
up the carriage, my strained Mandarin
swallowing one word in twelve,

to talk of the woes of a city
to a child, to talk of the woes…
Habitual speech that requires

no rehearsal in the equation of
need, the star-encrusted notes tight
in those gloveless, hugging paws.

What kind of accomplice am I,
placing nothing in this child's hands,
imagining the gangs and incredible

parents off-duty brawling, the other
guardians dead in the winter ground?
Charity in the sentimental houses,

those nearest to them giving,
individuals of high net worth giving –
if they can bring themselves – what?

What is it they give? I have taken
from the power of equations a guardian,
if there is a pacific speech to give.

Urban and Urbane

Black cars in the official lanes.
The depth of their shadows

is the depth of purpose
refracted beyond light.

Your building sites are
preparations of war

in the foundations
among rusted satellites.

This is how we grow:
from conception to power

through disappointment
of the underestimated,

the underestimated
creating night.

Faces that know graft
as the weather know this:

that it does not change
black cars in the official lanes.

No one sees their arrivals
and those that may are deprived

of vision which comes not
in change or the changing guards

staring but in the eloquence
of attention, of uncreated night

that is attentive and now once
more disappointing and real.

The Poetry of Impetuous Fish

is very quick
as in the gill-snatched breath.

The hook in my cheek
slung overboard for meat

bleeds for our orations
which in polished scales

of the length of my tail
defeats the water-weight.

A flash of iridescent life
thrown back

in the rapids

so very late

Becoming Silent

The expenditure of speaking
keeps its books in the coffers
of breathing and has its price.

There is a kind of extravagance
in becoming silent, if willed,
for the cost of falling silent.

I have heard men of power
cleave desire from fear.
Nothing remains but the petrified,

as if to say the petrified
nothing remains, which is
too elegant to be silent.

Say the ungifted reassure
themselves of reality's debts
through perpetual noise.

You must make silence
from out of your words
become the clearest auditor

now the skyline is also becoming
emptier, inelegant and the city also
within your breathing as if it is.

A Postcard from Peter Reading

i.m. Peter Reading (1946-2011)

I

Postmarked 'Shropshire, 1993,'
February or September:
the initial letters eroded now.

Incongruously enveloped,
by First Class mail,
slim, used brown,

overlaid with which
a sticker from
Friends of the Earth

reads:

Envelope re-use labels.
Friends of the Earth are campaigning on:

Tropical Rainforests,
The Ozone Layer,
The Green House Effect,

Water Pollution, Pesticides,
Safe Energy and
Cities for People…

though I'd no idea, then,
you'd already traipsed
through *Water and Waste.*

Underneath that label
I can still discern, faintly,
your home address.

II

Incongruously enveloped
until the postcard unsheathed
reveals your generous,

expansive hand covering
the entire white space
like a canvas primed.

And on the reverse
a reproduction of Weekes'
The Pig's Picnic.

Then this:

Dear Edward,

*It was good to meet you the other week. I'm a different chap since I
visited Oundle (I've put childish things aside and decided to become a
grown up).*

*You won't catch me at this address for much longer. I'm going into exile
(domestic collapse – 'tis an oft told tale) and will soon be living in a
barrel like Diogenes, the Cynic.*

Best wishes,

Peter Reading

At the head:

Overleaf: Due to unforeseen circumstances lunch will be delayed by ≈
24 hours.

Weekes' huge black sow
nosing toward a lobster,
the young servant boy

drowsing supine,
a white handkerchief
upon his face,

scene from that fiction
of fictions: a sweltering
English summer's day.

His top hat behind him:
sleeping, or out of it,
for in the bottom left

(almost your vinous signature)
a wine bottle lies on its side,
its neck hidden from the eye,

as if for this servant boy
(as for MacNeice) the morning
after was the first day.

Above him to the back left
the picnic party is arriving,
a lady's parasol,

a gentleman's top hat,
courtship of a feast
shortly to be devoured.

At the top right, a party
of ravenous boar hell-smelt
on that sow's crustacean

and crusted pie and
cold cuts who, thus
far, has merely upset

one white place set.
They will arrive upon
the boy drowsing supine,

but for now the schoolboy
turns your postcard
in his hands

(incongruously enveloped),
a kindness I suspect
some of your readers

dare not nor could not know,
The Telegraph obit
grudgingly applauding

how your melancholic 'lows'
took *the tradition of British
miserabilism to new heights*...

Could you have seen
my Chinese students
fall about laughing

at *Fiction*, 'Don' and Donald,
your *nom de plumes*,
your essential reading.

III

Twenty years on
from your first final poems
(bowing first final farewells),

this post-dated epitaph
I cannot inscribe, even
for a hand steeped in wine,

but haul the *vendange tardive*
of unforeseen circumstances
to begin,

67

begin with a poet's kindness,
who, with broken leg,
hobbled down my teacher's

stairs and hobbled back
to a pokey first-floor flat
considering a sixteen year-old's

poems, neither to poke nor jest,
sending me to *The New Princeton
Encylcopedia of Poetry and Poetics*

(then new) penning this postcard
on the back of a letter lost
to each our memories.

A poet's kindness...
whom I last saw
at King's Lynn two years on,

reading Auden's 'Musée des Beaux Arts'
knowing better than most
the genius of the old masters,

that there is the doggy life,
the torturer's horse
scratching its rump,

something amazing falling
from the sky
unnoticed by the expensive,

delicate ship which had
*somewhere to get to
and sailed calmly on*

as the merchants
pass Diogenes
in his barrel shored

up against that ruin,
in protest of coins and
the currencies

of circumstance.
From *Waste and Water*
clearing your throat

you said, of *Audenese*,
untying your bicycle clips
like Larkin – if not

church-going – to sing
in full-throated ease

of this England
and, without embarrassment,
of love besides.

Total Silence

To achieve it and
remain conscious,

which is the same…

For those who are dead
are no more conscious

of total silence
than the stones advising us.

Neither blood in the ears,
nor your heart thumping

at the wall, nor the car
in a country road,

nor even birds in flight
in the silentest mind

may approach it.

What little of speech
it also requires.

Erasure, they say,
is its death-knell.

But what is most there
is not deafening,

though there may be
no absence of sound.

Movement too is possible,
movements as of the body

in a car within country lanes
in silence moving.

To achieve it
and remain conscious

is peace,
that of which none may speak...

A Force That Takes

Each poem has its drama,
whether minuscule or minute,
wherein one voice

or another, the reader
at its table, the paper-weight
and impressing heel

become a force that takes.
The intellectuals and the merchants,
the currency between them.

Theirs is the larger drama
touching the minuscule,
or forced from there,

not prehensile, but feeding,
multiplying, digesting,
like the autolysis of yeast.

One has felt the force
of the offices and shipyards
and sheet metal,

another scorched words at a
study wall, the fury between
them, as a force that takes.

What I have in mind is
your comprehending touch,
waltz of a woman's hips,

that if the poem has
comprehended anything
it has told us, in so many

words, this is the force
that runs through it, this is
the minuscule we comprehend.

Beijing in Bright Spring Light

Willows of the Fourth Ring
sprout little shoots of green.

A girl idles in Chaoyang Park
flanked by a scampering toy dog

guiltless of impressions
or so we say.

The babies come
swaddled to near suffocation,

sweating in the new spring light
in immaculate pushchairs.

The unframed enthusiasm
of a child…

An old woman
beautiful in age

sucks the juice from
a peach insatiable,

travelling at remarkable
taxi-driven speeds.

It is impossible to desist
guiltless of impressions

though we are innocent
and may crave

the unframed enthusiasm
of a child:

which lives for us
in the ice-sculpted months

of memory or in laughter
unleashed upon a face

spontaneously in the
bright spring light amazing.

This England

I walked among millions
and sat in thousands
of miles of airline seats

returning to that first of lines,
(or near enough) boarding the train
from Newcastle, the colonnaded

arches of Durham and Darlington,
the bricked ramps,
vestigia of empire, then

(as we depart) the mines
and the factories gone
from ships to armaments

to the foot-ridden fields
in which an occasional horse
nods its answering flies.

The sky is turquoise tonight
and the clouds drawn upon
the ridge-backed hills

of this England
of which
I do not write…

whose earth is wet, even
damper than I remember,
vested in mulch and compost,

the singular acquisitions
of worms and moles
and water voles